PLAY GERSHWIN

C000138793

Solos for B♭ clarinet and piano

from songs by

GEORGE GERSHWIN

(1898-1937)

arranged by Alan Gout

FABER **𝆑𝆑** MUSIC

Contents

© 1997 by Faber Music Ltd
First published in 1997 by Faber Music Ltd
Bloomsbury House 74–77 Great Russell Street London WC1B 3DA
Music set by Barnes Music Engraving Ltd
Cover illustration © Brian Sweet
Printed in England by Caligraving Ltd
All rights reserved

ISBN10: 0-571-51754-4
EAN13: 978-0-571-51754-1

For copyright reasons, this edition is not for sale in the USA or Japan

To buy Faber Music publications or to find out about the full range of titles available
please contact your local music retailer or Faber Music sales enquiries:

Faber Music Ltd, Burnt Mill, Elizabeth Way, Harlow, Essex CM20 2HX
Tel: +44 (0)1279 82 89 82   Fax: +44 (0)1279 82 89 83
sales@fabermusic.com   fabermusicstore.com

They can't take that away from me

© 1997 by Faber Music Ltd

This music is copyright. Photocopying is illegal.

Oh, Lady be good

'S wonderful

A foggy day

Embraceable you

Bb CLARINET

PLAY GERSHWIN

Solos for Bb clarinet and piano from songs by

GEORGE GERSHWIN

(1898-1937)

arranged by Alan Gout

© 1997 by Faber Music Ltd
First published in 1997 by Faber Music Ltd
Bloomsbury House 74–77 Great Russell Street London WC1B 3DA
Music set by Barnes Music Engraving Ltd
Cover illustration © Brian Sweet
Printed in England by Caligraving Ltd
All rights reserved

ISBN10: 0-571-51754-4
EAN13: 978-0-571-51754-1

For copyright reasons, this edition is not for sale in the USA or Japan

To buy Faber Music publications or to find out about the full range of titles available
please contact your local music retailer or Faber Music sales enquiries:

Faber Music Ltd, Burnt Mill, Elizabeth Way, Harlow, Essex CM20 2HX
Tel: +44 (0)1279 82 89 82   Fax: +44 (0)1279 82 89 83
sales@fabermusic.com   fabermusicstore.com

FABER *ff* MUSIC

They can't take that away from me

© 1997 by Faber Music Ltd

This music is copyright. Photocopying is illegal.

Oh, Lady be good

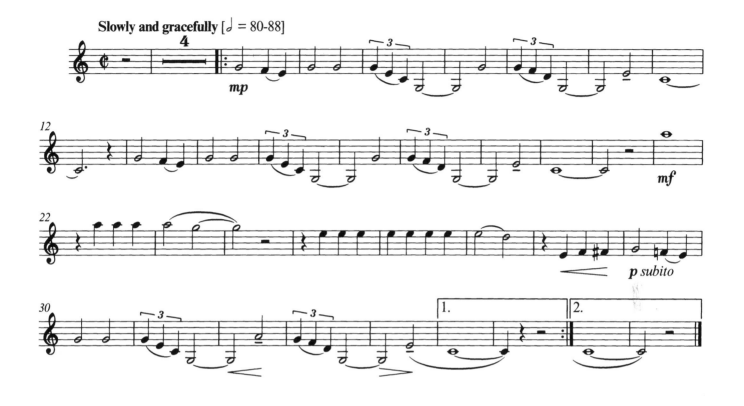

'S wonderful

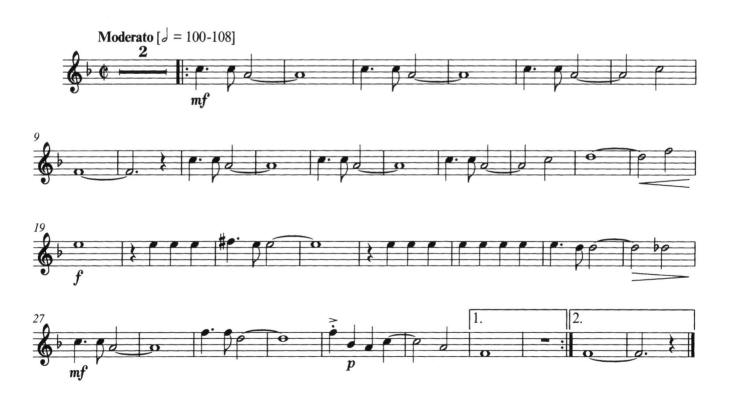

4

A foggy day

Embraceable you

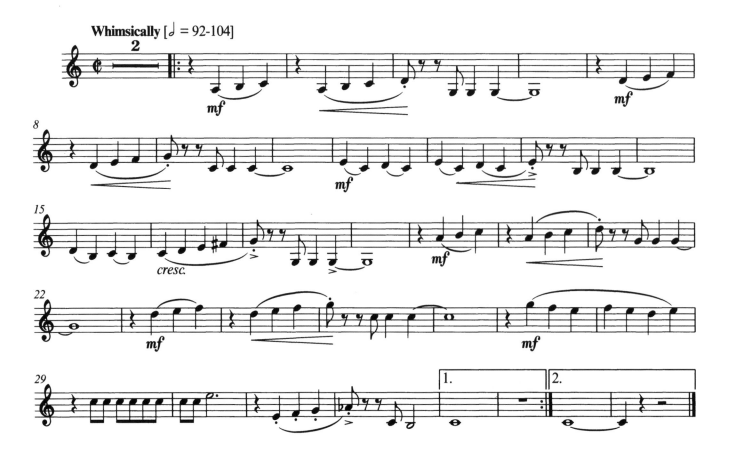

Summertime

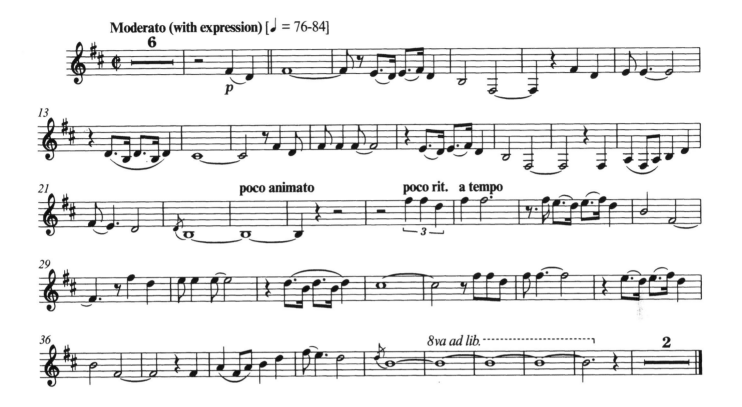

I got rhythm

It ain't necessarily so

Let's call the whole thing off

Bess, you is my woman now

Summertime

I got rhythm

It ain't necessarily so

Let's call the whole thing off

Bess, you is my woman now

Help with homework

English essentials

HI, MY NAME IS *KITCAT*...

... AND I'M *DIG*.

WE ARE HERE TO HELP YOU THROUGH THESE EXERCISES. START AT THE BEGINNING AND DON'T DO TOO MUCH IN ONE GO.

IT WON'T BE EASY ALL THE TIME – SOME PAGES CAN BE TRICKY – BUT WE'VE GIVEN YOU THE ANSWERS IN CASE YOU GET REALLY STUCK. NO PEEPING THOUGH! YOU WILL RECOGNISE A LOT OF THIS FROM THE WORK YOU DO AT SCHOOL (SORRY!). NOW DON'T YOU WISH YOU'D PAID MORE ATTENTION?! *GOOD LUCK!*

Written by Nina Filipek
Designed and illustrated by Dan Green
Cover design by Dan Green

www.autumnchildrensbooks.co.uk

know your nouns

stick a reward sticker here!

A **noun** is a person, place or thing.

The sentences below don't make sense because the nouns are incorrect. Cross out the noun (underlined) and replace it with a noun from the box.

1. I hurt my <u>hair</u>.   _____

2. The <u>river</u> is still wet.   _____

3. Don't touch the <u>clouds</u>!   _____

4. Red is my favourite <u>dish</u>.   _____

5. Can I have a <u>lion</u>?   _____

6. Let's go for a <u>sky</u>.   _____

Nouns:

walk	exhibits	paint
colour	biscuit	knee

A **collective noun** is a word given to a group of things, eg a **team** of footballers.

get it?

The word 'walk' can be a noun or a verb depending on how it is used in the sentence, eg 'a walk' is a noun but 'he walks' is a verb. If you can write 'a' or 'an' before the word then it is usually a noun.

Choose a collective noun from the list to complete these phrases.

1. a _____ of dolphins

2. a _____ of fish

3. a _____ of ants

4. a _____ of people

5. a _____ of stars

6. a _____ of ships

7. a _____ of eggs

8. a _____ of puppies

Collective nouns:

colony	pod	litter
fleet	shoal	galaxy
crowd	clutch	

DO YOU KNOW ANY OTHER COLLECTIVE NOUNS?